AROUND-THE-CLOCK EXCELLENCE

WINNING STRATEGIES FOR HOME CARE BUSINESS LEADERS

SAGE THOMPSON

Copyright © 2024 by Sage Thompson

All rights reserved.

No part of this publication may be reproduced, distributed, or transmitted in any form or by any means, including photocopying, recording, or other electronic or mechanical methods, without the prior written permission of the publisher, except in the case of brief quotations embodied in critical reviews and certain other noncommercial uses permitted by copyright law.

The information in this book is true and complete to the best of our knowledge. All recommendations are made without guarantee on the part of the author or publisher. The author and publisher disclaim any liability in connection with the use of information

Table of contents

INTRODUCTION **5**
   Welcome to Around-the-Clock Excellence............... 5
CHAPTER 1 .... **13**
ESTABLISHING THE BASE **13**
   Comprehending the Home Care Environment........13
   Clarifying Your Goals and Vision........................... 17
   Building a Strong Organizational Culture................23
CHAPTER 2 .... **29**
TACTICAL GUIDANCE **29**
   Successful Leadership Approaches in Home Care 29
   Hiring and Training Talent...................................... 36
   Sustainability and Financial Management.............. 43
CHAPTER 3 .... **51**
OPERATIONAL EXCELLENCE **51**
   Improving Functional Effectiveness........................ 51
   Strategies for Client-Centered Care....................... 58
   Problem-Solving and Crisis Management.............. 64
CHAPTER 4 .... **71**
DEVELOPMENT AND CREATIVITY **71**
   Promotion and Business Growth........................... 71
   Creative Solutions for Care....................................77
   Growing Your Company...83
CHAPTER 5 .... **91**
MAINTAINING GREATNESS **91**

    Ongoing Enhancement and Modification................91
    Durability and Legacy of Leadership...................... 98
CONCLUSION.. 105
    Your Path to Around-the-Clock Excellence...........105

INTRODUCTION

Welcome to Around-the-Clock Excellence

Greetings and welcome to "Around-the-Clock Excellence: Winning Strategies for Leaders in the Home Care Industry. This book is meant to serve as your all-inclusive guide through the intricacies of the home care sector, giving you the knowledge and resources you need to steer your company toward prosperity. This book will provide insightful tactics and useful guidance to improve your company's operations and leadership abilities, regardless of how experienced you are as a leader or how recently you entered the home care industry.

The Development of In-Home Assistance

Over the last several decades, there have been substantial changes in the home care business. What started out as a simple service to help the elderly and handicapped with everyday tasks has developed into a complex industry providing a broad variety of both medical and non-medical services. The complexity and expansion of home care have been fueled by changes in legislative frameworks, demographic shifts, and advancements in healthcare technology.

In the past, family members or inexperienced assistants were often in charge of providing home care. It's a career today, needing certain knowledge and abilities. Today's home care organizations provide customers with in-home services including physical therapy, professional nursing care, and chronic illness management.

Because more people are choosing to age in place, the need for home care services is predicted to grow as the population ages and medical developments allow for more care to be given outside of conventional hospital settings.

It is essential that executives in the home care sector comprehend this change. It emphasizes the need for ongoing education and adjustment in order to maintain competitiveness and satisfy customers' ever-changing requirements. Keep up with industry developments and trends to put your company in a position to succeed in this changing landscape.

The Value of Guidance in Home Care

Any home care company that wants to succeed must have strong leadership. As a leader, you shape the culture of your company, have an impact on the standard of service given, and determine the long-term course of your enterprise. Robust leadership is crucial to ensuring the survival and prosperity of your organization in an industry where mistakes may have devastating consequences.

In home care, leadership involves more than just overseeing employees and daily tasks. It entails promoting an environment that values kindness, brilliance, and ongoing development. It requires a thorough comprehension of the particular difficulties encountered by home care providers, such as maintaining high standards of care, overseeing regulatory compliance, and attending to the wide range of client demands.

In addition, proficient leaders stimulate and encourage their groups, fostering an atmosphere where staff members are involved, dedicated, and enabled to provide optimal healthcare services. Additionally, they place a great priority on continuing education and professional development to make sure that their staff members have the most up-to-date information and abilities to provide high-quality treatment.

You will get insights into a variety of leadership philosophies and techniques from this book, which will assist you in creating a leadership strategy that complements your personal beliefs and the demands of your company. The fundamentals of good leadership are the same whether you are in charge of a small team or a huge corporation: having a clear vision, being dedicated to excellence, and putting an emphasis on creating a supportive and productive work environment.

How to Get the Most Out of This Book

"Around-the-Clock Excellence" offers a combination of theoretical insights and doable tactics in an approachable and instructive manner. Here are some pointers for making the most of this book's advantages:

1. **Read Actively and Reflectively:** Spend some time considering how the ideas and tactics in each chapter relate to your own company as you go through it. To record your ideas, goals, and thoughts, think about maintaining a notebook.
2. **Interact with the Case Studies:** Throughout the book, there are case studies that show how the tactics described are used in actual situations. Make use of these case studies as a source

of motivation and to learn how others have handled comparable difficulties.

3. **Implement the methods:** This is a practical book with advice and methods unique to your company that you may use from chapter to chapter. Work your way gradually through the other parts, starting with the ones that are most pertinent to your requirements right now.

4. **Make Use of the Appendices:** The appendices include further resources, such as suggested tools, model business strategies, and supplementary reading lists. These tools are meant to assist you in continuing to learn and grow.

5. **Cultivate a Culture of Continuous Improvement:** Make use of the knowledge and techniques in this book to help your company develop a culture of

continuous improvement. As your team reads pertinent portions, have a discussion about how the ideas might be applied to their respective jobs.

6. **Join the Conversation:** The profession of leadership in home care is always changing. Participate in online forums, conferences, and professional networks to network with other industry experts. Talk about your experiences, take advice from others, and keep up with emerging trends and industry best practices.

You will be well-prepared to successfully run your home care company and achieve long-term success if you adhere to these recommendations. Keep in mind that this book is your travel companion as you pursue greatness around-the-clock.

CHAPTER 1

ESTABLISHING THE BASE

Comprehending the Home Care Environment

Industry Developments and Difficulties

Due to the aging population, improvements in medical technology, and the desire to age in place, the home care sector is expanding quickly. The number of Americans 65 and older is predicted to almost quadruple by 2050, which would raise the need for home care services. Home care has also undergone a revolution with technological developments like telehealth and remote monitoring, which enable high-quality care to be given to patients in the comfort of their own homes.

But these prospects also provide important obstacles. The lack of workers is one of the primary problems. There is a severe shortage of personnel due to the high turnover rates and increasing demand for home care providers. In addition, the sector is under financial strain from declining reimbursement rates and rising regulatory standard compliance expenses.

The need for ongoing education and training to stay up-to-date with the ever-evolving healthcare industry is another difficulty. To guarantee they are providing the best possible care, home care professionals need to remain up-to-date on the newest medical techniques, innovations, and industry best practices.

Compliance and the Regulatory Environment

Managing the regulatory landscape is essential to operating a home care company. To protect customers' safety and wellbeing, the home care sector is subject to strict regulations. State-by-state variations in regulations might include things like staffing ratios, background checks on potential hires, licensing requirements, and care standards compliance.

Adherence to these standards is vital and requires a comprehensive comprehension of the legal terrain. Frequent audits and inspections are conducted, and noncompliance may result in fines, penalties, or even the revocation of an operating license. As a result, it's critical to set up strong compliance systems and keep abreast of any modifications to laws.

A good tactic is to assign a compliance officer or team to keep an eye on any changes to regulations and make the appropriate modifications. Investing in compliance management software may also help to expedite this procedure and guarantee that your company continues to adhere to all applicable rules and regulations.

The Market Environment

There are many providers fighting for customers in the very competitive home care industry. It's difficult to stand out in such a crowded market unless you have a firm grasp of your rivals and the special value you provide.

Analyzing competitors is an important first step. Determine what makes your services unique and evaluate the advantages and disadvantages of your primary rivals. Do you provide specialist treatment that isn't provided by others? Do you have a track record of providing outstanding customer service? Make use of this data to hone your value proposition and emphasize the distinctive qualities of your company.

You may gain a competitive advantage by establishing solid ties with referral sources, including medical facilities, doctors' offices, and neighborhood associations. These alliances have the potential to bring you new business and improve your standing in the neighborhood.

Clarifying Your Goals and Vision

Formulating a Clearly Stated Vision

A vision statement is an effective tool for expressing your goals for your home care company's future. It gives you inspiration and guidance, influencing your strategic choices and inspiring your group. A strong vision statement should represent your long-term objectives and the desired influence on the community you serve in a clear, succinct, and forward-looking manner.

A vision statement may be something like this: "To be the leading provider of high-quality, compassionate home care services, improving the lives of our clients and their families."

When creating your vision statement, think about the goals you have for your company and the fundamental principles that guide it. Involve your staff in this process to make sure that everyone in your company understands your vision and is motivated to work together to achieve it.

Defining Fundamental Principles

The guiding ideas and ideals that direct the choices and activities of your business are known as core values. They help to define the culture of your business, impact how you communicate with customers and staff, and provide a framework for formulating strategic choices.

Consider the things that are most important to your company while establishing your core principles. In home care, common core values might include compassion, excellence, honesty, and respect. Once your values have been determined, make sure your staff is aware of them and incorporate them into all facets of your company's operations, including recruiting procedures and customer interactions.

If compassion is one of your fundamental values, for instance, make sure that your recruiting process reflects this by selecting candidates that exhibit empathy and a sincere desire to assist others. In a similar vein, make sure your training programs reflect company values by stressing the significance of compassionate care in each and every client engagement.

Establishing both short-term and long-term goals

To turn your vision and ideals into doable actions, you must set objectives. Setting goals gives your company a path forward by assisting with resource allocation, activity prioritization, and progress tracking.

Establish long-term objectives that support your vision first. These may include reaching a certain income goal, growing your clientele, or extending your service area. Long-term objectives have to be challenging but doable, offering a clear path for the growth and improvement of your company.

Next, decompose your long-term aims into manageable short-term targets. These need to be SMART goals—specific, measurable, realistic, pertinent, and time-bound. If your long-term aim is to increase the size of your service area, for instance, your short-term goal may be to build a new office within the following year in a nearby city.

Make sure your objectives are still in line with your vision and your company's changing requirements by reviewing and adjusting them on a regular basis. Honor your accomplishments and see any losses as chances to grow and learn.

Building a Strong Organizational Culture

Promoting a Positive Workplace Culture

Enhancing job happiness, recruiting and keeping talented workers, and raising overall performance all depend on a healthy work environment. Establishing a climate of mutual respect, cooperation, and acknowledgment is the first step.

Promote transparent communication and provide avenues for staff members to express their thoughts, worries, and suggestions. Tools that may help promote open communication include anonymous surveys, suggestion boxes, and regular team meetings.

Acknowledgment is also essential. Honor your staff members' accomplishments and efforts with rewards, team gatherings, or handwritten messages of gratitude. Motive and morale may be greatly increased by praising and recognizing effort and commitment.

Promoting Honest Conversation

A robust company culture is based on effective communication. It guarantees that all members of the team are in agreement, minimizes miscommunication, and cultivates a feeling of oneness among them.

Create unambiguous official and informal communication routes. Regular team meetings, one-on-one check-ins, and an open-door policy for the leadership are a few examples of this. Encourage staff members to share their thoughts and provide criticism without worrying about consequences.

Additionally, transparency is crucial. Inform your workforce of significant choices, adjustments, and advancements happening inside the company. This promotes trust and makes sure that each person feels important and is participating.

Methods for Increasing Staff Engagement and Retention

Employees who are engaged in their work produce more, provide greater care, and are less likely to quit. The following are some methods to improve worker retention and engagement:

1. **Provide Opportunities for Professional Development:** To assist your staff members in developing and advancing in

their professions, provide training courses, seminars, and chances for ongoing education. This shows your dedication to their professional growth while also improving their abilities.

2. **Create a supportive work environment:** Make sure your staff members have the tools and assistance they need to do their tasks well. This entails maintaining appropriate personnel numbers, providing attractive pay and benefits, and encouraging a healthy work-life balance.

3. **Cultivate a Sense of Purpose:** Assist your staff in connecting with the goals and principles of your company. Demonstrate to them how their efforts improve the quality of life for customers and their families. Employee motivation and commitment are more likely to be present

when they are aware of the effects of their job.

4. **Ask for and act on feedback:** Ask your staff members often about their work happiness, difficulties, and recommendations for development. Utilize this input to resolve any problems and implement improvements within your company.

5. **Encourage team building and collaboration:** Provide chances for workers to work together and form connections, as well as support team-building exercises. A supportive work environment and increased job satisfaction may be fostered by a strong feeling of camaraderie.

By concentrating on these tactics, you can create a powerful company culture that draws and keeps top talent, raises employee engagement, and eventually improves customer results.

You establish a strong foundation for your home care firm by comprehending the home care landscape, clearly articulating your vision and goal, and creating a strong organizational culture. These components are essential for overcoming industry obstacles, setting yourself apart in a crowded market, and seeing long-term success.

CHAPTER 2

TACTICAL GUIDANCE

Successful Leadership Approaches in Home Care

Determining Your Leadership Approach

Strategic thinking, empathy, and a special combination of abilities are needed for leadership in home care. Being a successful leader starts with knowing your style of leadership. There are various common leadership styles, each having its own benefits and weaknesses:

1. **Autocratic Leadership:** Autocratic leaders tend to act alone and don't consult their team members too much. In emergency circumstances where quick

decision-making is essential, this approach may work well. However, if used excessively, it could result in poor staff morale and high turnover.

2. **Democratic Leadership:** Members of a Democratic team participate in decision-making. This strategy encourages teamwork and may result in more inventiveness and employee happiness. It could, however, cause decision-making to lag.

3. **Transformational Leadership:** Leaders who embody this style inspire and encourage their team to go above and beyond expectations. Their main goals are to establish a culture of continual development and to create a vision for the future. This approach works especially well in home care, where empowering and

motivating staff members may result in better care.

4. **Transactional Leadership:** Transactional leaders prioritize structure, oversight, and incentives and penalties based on output. While this approach could be useful for achieving short-term objectives and preserving consistency, it might not foster innovation or long-term loyalty.

5. **Servant Leadership:** Servant leaders put their team and customers' needs first. They provide an exemplary example and concentrate on creating a welcoming and inclusive atmosphere. This approach works effectively in home care, where compassion and encouragement are crucial.

Consider your innate inclinations and decision-making process to determine your leadership style. Get input from your group, and think about using leadership evaluation instruments. By being aware of your style, you can make the most of your advantages and enhance any areas that need work.

Modifying Your Strategy for Various Circumstances

Good leaders are aware that no two situations are the same. Various circumstances call for various leadership philosophies. For instance, in order to act quickly in a crisis, an authoritarian approach may be required. On the other hand, a transformative or democratic strategy could work better for long-term planning.

Being adaptable and sensitive to the demands of your team and the current circumstances are key components of changing your leadership approach. Take into account these suggestions:

- **Assess the Situation:** Consider the situation's possible significance, intricacy, and urgency. This will assist you in choosing the best leadership strategy.
- **Know Your Team:** Recognize the advantages, disadvantages, and inclinations of the people on your team. You may use this information to help you decide which leadership style is appropriate for a certain situation.
- **Communicate Clearly:** Effective communication is crucial, regardless of the approach you use. Make sure everyone on your team is aware of your

expectations and the reasoning behind your choices.

- **Be Consistent but Flexible:** Although maintaining consistency is crucial for fostering trust, be prepared to modify your strategy when necessary. You may handle shifting conditions and accomplish higher results by being flexible.

Case Studies of Effective Executives

Getting knowledge and inspiration from accomplished home care business professionals may be very beneficial. The following three case studies include influential leaders:

The Transformational Leader: Case Study 1

Caring Hands Home Care's CEO, Jane Smith, turned a failing home care company into a profitable enterprise. Her main goals were establishing a common goal and encouraging a constant development mindset. Employee engagement and customer satisfaction were raised by Jane by empowering her team and fostering creativity. Her staff was motivated by her leadership to go above and beyond, which greatly increased the agency's development and prominence.

The Servant Leader: Case Study 2

Compassionate Care Services' founder, John Doe, based his company on the ideas of servant leadership. John sets a positive example for his team members and customers by prioritizing their well-being and fostering a positive work atmosphere. His strategy produced a high level of staff loyalty and retention, which translated into great customer service. John gained a reputation as a kind and capable leader because of his dedication to his group and clientele.

The Democratic Leader: Case Study 3

Emily Johnson, Home Comfort Care's director of operations, included her staff in decision-making by using a democratic leadership style. She appreciated the opinions of her staff members and often asked for their ideas. This cooperative approach produced creative fixes and enhanced procedures. The success of the business was facilitated by Emily's leadership style, which instilled in her staff a feeling of responsibility and ownership.

Hiring and Training Talent

Top Techniques for Recruiting Excellent Talent

Hiring excellent people is essential to providing superior in-home care services. The following are some top strategies for drawing in and selecting the top applicants:

1. **Create Clearly Definable Job Descriptions:** Clearly describe the duties, responsibilities, and skills needed for every job. This draws in applicants who are qualified for the position.
2. **Use multiple recruitment outlets:** post job openings on social media, professional networks, and online job boards, among other outlets. To identify suitable applicants, think about collaborating with nearby educational institutions and training initiatives.

3. **Examine Candidates Detailed:** Check references and do extensive background checks. Conduct organized interviews to evaluate the qualifications, background, and cultural fit of applicants.

4. **Highlight Your Company Culture:** In your job advertisements and during interviews, highlight the values, purpose, and culture of your company. A corporation whose ideals coincide with the candidate's own is likely to draw them in.

5. **Offer Competitive Benefits and Compensation:** Make sure your benefit packages are competitive for the sector. Think about providing extra perks like wellness initiatives, professional development opportunities, and flexible scheduling.

6. **Streamline the recruiting process:** Try to streamline and make the recruiting process as transparent and easy as you can. Maintain constant contact with applicants and provide prompt comments.

Programs for Training and Development

Maintaining a trained and motivated staff requires investing in training and development. The following are some crucial methods for developing successful training initiatives:

1. **Orientation and Onboarding:** Offer new personnel thorough orientation and onboarding programs. Together with job-specific training, this should contain an overview of the rules, practices, and culture of your company.

2. **Continuous Training:** Provide staff with frequent training opportunities to stay up to speed on the newest technology, best practices, and legal needs. Webinars, seminars, and online courses might be examples of this.

3. **Coaching and Mentoring:** Assign new hires to seasoned mentors who can provide direction and assistance. Employees may further their careers and enhance their skill sets by participating in coaching programs.

4. **Professional Development:** Motivate staff members to seek professional certifications and ongoing education. Give time off and financial assistance for pertinent conferences and courses.

5. **Performance Evaluation and Feedback:** Conduct frequent performance evaluations

to pinpoint areas in need of improvement and provide helpful criticism. Using the results of these assessments, create individual growth plans for every worker.

6. **Leadership Training:** Provide courses on leadership to get staff members ready for managerial positions. Courses on team management, communication, and leadership are examples of this.

Developing a Route for Professional Growth

Maintaining top talent and employee motivation requires clearly defined career growth options. The following are some tactics to assist staff members in developing their careers within your company:

1. **Career Pathways:** Create well-defined career trajectories that delineate the

necessary actions and qualifications to progress to elevated roles. Share these routes with your staff, and make sure they have the tools and assistance they need.

2. **Skill Development:** Provide training courses aimed at enhancing the abilities needed for work at a higher level. To develop experience, encourage staff members to take on new tasks and responsibilities.

3. **Internal Promotions:** Whenever feasible, give internal promotions precedence over external hiring. Employees who do very well or have great potential should be acknowledged and rewarded.

4. **Succession Planning:** Put succession planning into practice to find and train candidates for important leadership

positions. This guarantees stability and continuity in your company.

5. **Recognition and Awards:** Give staff members credit for their accomplishments and efforts. Bonuses, job advancements, and public recognition of their work are a few examples of this.

6. **Career Counseling:** Assist staff members in identifying their objectives and creating a strategy to achieve them by offering career counseling and assistance. One-on-one meetings with managers or HR specialists may fall into this category.

Sustainability and Financial Management

Financial Planning and Budgeting

Good money management is essential to your home care business's viability and expansion. The following are some essential financial planning and budgeting techniques:

1. **Create a Comprehensive Budget:** List all of your anticipated spending and revenue in a comprehensive budget. Add subcategories for things like marketing, overhead, salary, and supplies. Review and revise your budget on a regular basis to account for changes in your company.

2. **Monitor Cash Flow:** Make sure you have enough money to pay your bills by keeping a careful check on your cash flow. Cash flow statements are a useful tool for monitoring your revenue and expenses and spotting any problems.

3. **Control Costs:** Reduce needless spending by putting cost-control strategies into place. This may include using technology to expedite processes, improving workforce levels, and haggling for lower prices from vendors.
4. **Prepare for Emergencies:** Put money away for unforeseen costs and crises. This might assist you in overcoming financial obstacles without endangering your company.
5. **Seek Professional Advice:** To create and oversee your financial strategy, think about collaborating with an accountant or financial counselor. They may provide insightful information and support you in making wise choices.

Cash Flow Management

Effective management of cash flow is essential to preserving the financial stability of your home care company. Here are some pointers for efficient cash flow management:

1. **Track Receivables:** Monitor your accounts receivable and pursue any unpaid balances. Establish a system that will allow you to remember and bill customers on time.
2. **Optimize payment arrangements:** Work out advantageous arrangements for suppliers and customers. This may include extending the deadline for payments or providing incentives for prompt payments.
3. **Maintain a Cash Reserve:** Put away a certain amount of your earnings for

emergencies. This might act as a buffer in times of need or slowness.

4. **Use technology:** Track your revenue and spending in real time by using accounting software. This might assist you in seeing patterns and coming to wise judgments.

5. **Monitor Expenses:** Examine your spending on a regular basis to find any areas where you might make savings. This may include contract renegotiation, waste reduction, and supplier sourcing that is more economical.

Finance and Investing Techniques

Getting financing and making wise investments are critical to your home care business's expansion and long-term viability. Here are some tactics to think about:

1. **Investigate Money Sources:** Examine several sources of money, including grants, bank loans, and venture capital. To decide which course of action is best for your company, think about consulting a financial expert.

2. **Create Relationships with Investors:** Make connections and cultivate a relationship with possible investors. Join groups for professionals and go to industry events to meet investors interested in the home care business.

3. **Write a Strong Business Plan:** Construct a thorough business plan that includes your objectives, tactics, and projected financials. This may aid in luring financiers and obtaining money.

4. **Invest in Technology:** Make an investment in technology that can raise

standards of care and increase productivity. These may include telemedicine platforms, scheduling software, and electronic health records.

5. **Diversify Your Services:** To draw in more customers and boost sales, broaden your scope of offerings. This may include providing extra support services, wellness initiatives, and specialized treatment.

6. **Pay Attention to Marketing:** Make investments in marketing plans to advertise your products and draw in new customers. Online advertising, neighborhood outreach, and referral schemes are a few examples of this.

You may set up your home care company for long-term success by using strong financial management techniques, hiring and developing top staff, and adopting successful leadership styles. In addition to leading your group and overseeing daily tasks, strategic leadership entails making long-term plans and seeing to it that your company is viable. You may guide your home care company to success in a cutthroat and always changing market by being flexible, learning new things on a regular basis, and being dedicated to quality work.

CHAPTER 3

OPERATIONAL EXCELLENCE

Improving Functional Effectiveness

Simplifying Procedures

Maintaining cost-effectiveness while providing superior home care services requires operational efficiency. Simplifying procedures is essential to reaching this level of effectiveness. To begin, sketch out your present procedures and look for any inefficiencies, redundancies, or bottlenecks. Engage your staff in this process to get a thorough perspective and receive their feedback on areas that might have improvement.

1. **Standardize Procedures:** To guarantee consistency and minimize mistakes,

establish precise, standardized processes for routine work. Make sure all employees are aware of and able to adhere to these processes by developing comprehensive policies and training materials.

2. **Workflow Optimization:** Examine processes in workflows to find areas where they may be optimized or removed. You may save time and lessen the stress on your personnel by, for instance, automating repetitive operations or merging similar jobs.

3. **Employee Training:** To make sure staff members are prepared to function effectively, regularly teach them new processes and best practices. Employees with proper training may complete jobs faster and with fewer errors, increasing output overall.

4. **Resource Allocation:** Make sure that personnel, tools, and supplies are distributed efficiently. Utilize data to determine peak hours and modify personnel numbers to match demand without going overboard at slower times.
5. **Continuous Improvement:** Encourage employees to make suggestions for process enhancements in order to cultivate a culture of continuous improvement. Maintaining the currentness and efficacy of processes requires regular reviews and updates.

Making Use of Automation and Technology

The optimization of operational efficiency in home care is mostly dependent on technology and automation. You may increase care quality, decrease administrative workloads, and expedite processes by using the newest hardware and software.

1. **Electronic Health Records (EHRs):** Use EHR systems to consolidate patient data and provide all personnel with easy access to it. EHRs may improve communication between caregivers and healthcare professionals, cut down on paperwork, and eliminate mistakes.
2. **Scheduling Software:** To handle employee assignments and customer appointments more effectively, use scheduling software. By using these technologies, you can make sure that the correct customers are paired with the proper caregivers, cut down on travel time, and optimize routes.

3. **Telehealth Solutions:** Combine telehealth systems to provide monitoring and consultations from a distance. This may improve the quality of treatment, particularly for patients with long-term illnesses or those who reside far away.
4. **Automation Tools:** Manage inventories, payroll, and other administrative duties automatically. Staff members may have more time to devote to high-priority duties like client care as a result.
5. **Data Analytics:** To learn more about your operations, use data analytics. To see patterns and come to wise judgments, examine financial data, customer feedback, and performance indicators.

Performance Measurements and Quality Assurance

Sustaining a high level of care is necessary to make your home care company successful. You can make sure that your services continuously meet or surpass customer expectations by putting in place a strong quality assurance procedure and monitoring performance indicators.

1. **Set Quality Standards:** Clearly define the standards of quality that apply to every facet of your business, including customer service and clinical treatment. Make sure that every employee is aware of these requirements.
2. **Regular Audits:** To evaluate adherence to quality standards, conduct audits and inspections on a regular basis. To assess performance and pinpoint areas in need of

development, use scorecards and checklists.

3. **Client Feedback:** Gather input from clients and their families in order to determine their level of satisfaction and pinpoint any problems. To get this data, do focus groups, interviews, and surveys.

4. **Performance Metrics:** Monitor important performance indicators, including response times, customer satisfaction ratings, and caregiver retention rates. Examine these indicators on a regular basis to track results and spot patterns.

5. **Continuous Training:** Make sure your employees have access to chances for professional growth and continuous training to keep them up to date on industry standards and best practices.

6. **Corrective Actions:** Establish a procedure for resolving any problems found in audits or feedback. Create action plans to address issues and stop them from happening again.

Strategies for Client-Centered Care

Recognizing the needs and expectations of the client

Understanding your customers' wants and expectations in depth is the first step towards providing client-centered service. This entails attending to their emotional, social, and personal needs in addition to their physical ones.

1. **Comprehensive Assessments:** Take the time to thoroughly evaluate prospective customers in order to learn about their

personal preferences, medical history, and present state of health. Incorporate feedback from patients, their relatives, and medical professionals.

2. **Regular Check-Ins:** Arrange for frequent check-ins with clients and their families to go over care plans, resolve issues, and make necessary service adjustments. This makes it possible to maintain care that meets their requirements and expectations.

3. **Cultural Competence:** Ensure that your employees are able to treat customers from a variety of backgrounds with respect and individual attention by training them in cultural competence. Communication may be enhanced, and the customer experience can be improved by acknowledging cultural variations.

4. **Personalized Care Plans:** Create customized care plans that take into account the particular requirements and preferences of every client. Engage clients and their families in the process of care planning so that their opinions are taken into account.

5. **Compassion and Empathy:** Motivate caregivers to show compassion and empathy while interacting with clients. Developing solid, dependable connections may improve the wellbeing and contentment of your clients.

Providing Personalized Attention

Meeting the various requirements of home care customers requires personalized treatment. Customizing services for each customer may enhance results and increase client satisfaction.

1. **Flexible Scheduling:** Provide customers with alternatives for flexible scheduling that suit their schedules and preferences. This may include scheduling care during certain times of the day or modifying visitation schedules.
2. **Client Preferences:** Be mindful of the preferences of your customers with relation to daily activities, nutrition, and care regimens. Urge caregivers to become knowledgeable about these preferences and apply them to their care.
3. **Specialized Services:** Offer tailored services to address certain needs, including dementia care for clients or post-operative rehabilitation for patients. Services that are customized to each client's requirements may enhance results and quality of life.

4. **Holistic Approach:** Provide treatment that takes into account the demands of the patient's physical, emotional, and social needs. This may involve engaging in mental health, social, and physical health-promoting activities.

5. **Family Involvement:** Include family members in the process of providing care so that they are knowledgeable and able to assist. Collaboration and regular contact with family members may improve the quality of treatment received overall.

Assessing Customer Contentment

In order to make sure that your services satisfy your customers' demands and to pinpoint areas that need improvement, it is essential to measure client satisfaction.

1. **Satisfaction Surveys:** Provide customers and their families with satisfaction surveys on a regular basis. To get thorough input, combine quantitative and qualitative questions.
2. **Client conversations:** To get more in-depth details about the experiences of your clients, have one-on-one conversations with them and their families. This may provide important information that surveys would miss.
3. **Feedback Mechanisms:** Provide a variety of avenues for customers to provide input, including suggestion boxes, online forms, and phone lines specifically designated for this purpose. Make it simple for customers to express their ideas and worries.
4. **Analyze Data:** Examine feedback data to find patterns and recurring problems.

Make well-informed judgments on how to modify and enhance your services using the information provided here.

5. **Acknowledge Feedback:** Demonstrate to customers that you appreciate their opinions by responding to their queries and recommendations. Share any updates or modifications brought forth by their suggestions.

Problem-Solving and Crisis Management

Formulating a Crisis Management Strategy

A strong crisis response strategy is necessary to handle crises and guarantee the security and welfare of your employees and customers.

1. **Risk Assessment:** To detect possible crises like natural catastrophes, medical

problems, or personnel shortages, do a comprehensive risk assessment. Take into account each risk's effect and probability.

2. **Emergency Procedures:** Create precise emergency protocols for many kinds of situations. Protocols for medical response, communication, evacuation, and continuity of care should all be part of this.

3. **Training and exercises:** To make sure your employees are ready to react appropriately, regularly teach them emergency protocols and hold exercises. This might include communication exercises, evacuation drills, and first aid training.

4. **Communication strategy:** Create a strategy outlining the dissemination of information in the event of a catastrophe.

Contact lists, routes of communication, and procedures for informing clients and family should all be part of this.

5. **Resource Allocation:** Make sure you have enough supplies, backup power, and personnel on hand to handle any emergencies. Make a plan for the distribution and use of these resources.

Practical Methods for Solving Issues

Good problem-solving abilities are necessary to handle daily difficulties and guarantee seamless operations.

1. **Identify the problem:** Clearly state the issue and collect all pertinent data. Involve important parties in order to fully comprehend the problem.

2. **Analyze the reasons:** To determine the underlying reasons for the issue, use techniques like root cause analysis. Rather than only treating the symptoms, this may assist you in addressing the problem at its root.
3. **Generate Solutions:** Discuss possible answers with your group. Promote original thought and weigh many choices before selecting the best path of action.
4. **Evaluate Options:** Determine the viability, dangers, and possible outcomes of every option. Take into account elements like the needed resources, time, and cost.
5. **Implement the Solution:** Assign duties and create a thorough execution strategy. Make certain that everyone who needs to

know is informed and participating in the process.

6. **Monitor and Adjust:** Keep an eye on the solution's efficacy and make any required modifications. Get input from your group and customers to be sure the issue has been fixed.

Taking Lessons from the Past

By thinking back on and gaining knowledge from previous mistakes, you may enhance your business processes and avoid repeating the same mistakes.

1. **Post-Mortem Analysis:** Following the resolution of a significant problem or crisis, carry out a post-mortem analysis. Get feedback from everyone who was

involved to find out what worked and what might have been done better.

2. **Record Lessons Learned:** Share with your team the lessons you've learned from previous difficulties. This may contribute to building a knowledge foundation that is future-ready.

3. **Update processes:** Revise your protocols and processes based on the knowledge you've gathered from previous difficulties. Make sure your staff is informed of any changes and that they are included in training materials.

4. **Cultivate a Learning Culture:** Promote an environment where learning and development are ongoing. Acknowledge and thank team members who make contributions to process improvement and issue solutions.

5. **frequent reviews:** Plan on reviewing previous problems and how they were fixed on a frequent basis. This may guarantee that gains are maintained over time and serve to reinforce lessons learned.

You may attain operational excellence in your home care company by concentrating on maximizing operational efficiency, providing client-centered care, and skillfully handling emergencies and issues. These tactics not only raise the standard of care but also increase your organization's overall sustainability and efficiency. By means of continuous enhancement and dedication to quality, you may guarantee the prosperity of your in-home care enterprise and provide outstanding care to your clientele.

CHAPTER 4

DEVELOPMENT AND CREATIVITY

Promotion and Business Growth

Developing an Effective Marketing Plan

Developing a successful marketing plan is crucial to expanding your home care company. A well-thought-out plan can assist you in expanding your clientele, strengthening your brand, and setting yourself apart from rivals.

1. **Identify Your Ideal Clientele:** Recognize your ideal clientele. Take into account factors related to age, geography, health, and income. You may increase the relevance and effect of your message by

focusing your marketing efforts on certain markets.

2. **Create your USP:** Determine what makes your home care company unique from the competition. Your USP needs to be the cornerstone of your marketing plan, whether it's unique services, first-rate customer support, or creative care solutions.

3. **Produce Interesting Content:** Write articles that speak to the interests and worries of your intended readership. Client testimonials, infographics, videos, and blog entries may all fall into this category. Content ought to show off your experience and be interesting and educational.

4. **Utilize multiple avenues:** Use email marketing, social media, conventional

advertising, and other avenues to reach your audience. Since every medium has advantages, you may increase your reach by using a diverse strategy.

5. **Measure and Adjust:** Use metrics like website traffic, lead generation, and conversion rates to regularly monitor the success of your marketing campaigns. Over time, make use of this data to hone your approach and get better outcomes.

Making Use of Digital Marketing Resources

Digital marketing tools may greatly improve your marketing efforts by expanding your audience reach and facilitating customer engagement.

1. **Search Engine Optimization (SEO):** To increase your online presence, make sure

your website and content are optimized for search engines. This involves making sure your website is mobile-friendly, employing pertinent keywords, and producing material of the highest quality.

2. **Pay-Per-Click (PPC) Advertising:** Increase targeted website traffic using PPC advertising. You can monitor the effectiveness of your campaigns and target certain demographics using platforms like Google advertisements and social media advertisements.

3. **Social Media Marketing:** Make use of social media channels to establish a connection with prospective customers and develop your brand. To reach a larger audience, provide insightful material, interact with them, and take advantage of paid advertising.

4. **Email Marketing:** Utilize your email list to cultivate connections with prospective customers. To keep your audience interested and informed, send out newsletters, updates, and special offers on a regular basis.
5. **Analytics Tools:** Monitor the results of your digital marketing campaigns with the help of analytics tools. To assist you in improving in improving your plan, Google Analytics, social media insights, and email marketing analytics may provide useful data.

Constructing robust robust referral referral systems systems

Networks of referrals are an effective tool for expanding your home care company. Developing connections with local businesses, healthcare professionals, and happy customers may lead to a constant flow of recommendations.

1. **Healthcare Providers:** Make connections with physicians, nurses, and discharge coordinators from hospitals. Tell them about your offerings and how you can support their patients.
2. **Community Organizations:** Form alliances with neighborhood non-profits, churches, and senior centers. These groups often collaborate closely with people who may need home care services.
3. **Client Testimonials:** Urge happy customers to recommend your services to their friends and relatives. To encourage them, provide rewards like discounts or bonuses for referring others.

4. **Professional Networks:** To network with other professionals, go to industry events and become a member of professional organizations. Developing connections with other in-home caregivers may also increase the chances of referrals.
5. **Continuous Follow-Up:** Stay in touch with the people who recommended you. To keep your company front of mind, publish success stories and provide updates on your services.

Creative Solutions for Care

Combining Remote Monitoring and Telehealth

With new methods for delivering care and keeping an eye on clients' health, telehealth and remote monitoring are revolutionizing the home care sector.

1. **Telehealth Consultations:** Make telehealth services available to conduct follow-up visits and virtual consultations. Care access may be enhanced by this, particularly for patients who live far away or have mobility challenges.
2. **Remote Monitoring Devices:** Monitor the health metrics and vital signs of your customers using remote monitoring devices. Caregivers may get real-time data from devices like wearable fitness trackers, glucose meters, and blood pressure monitors.
3. **Data Integration:** Connect your electronic health records (EHR) system to telehealth and remote monitoring data. This guarantees that caregivers and healthcare practitioners have easy access to all pertinent information.

4. **Client Education:** Inform clients and their families about the uses and advantages of remote monitoring and telehealth. Give them assistance and training so they can get used to the technology.
5. **Continuous Improvement:** Regularly assess how well your remote monitoring and telehealth initiatives are working. Get input from caregivers and clients to determine what needs to be improved.

Investigating novel novel care care models models

You can keep ahead of market trends and satisfy your customers' changing requirements by using innovative service models.

1. **Integrated Care:** Create integrated care models that facilitate the coordination of services across various providers and environments. For patients with complex requirements, this may enhance health outcomes and the continuity of treatment.
2. **Client-Centered Care:** Put into practice client-centered care models that give clients' needs and preferences first priority. Client participation in care planning and decision-making is part of this.
3. **PreventativePreventative Care:** To assist clients in maintaining their health and avoiding hospitalizations, prioritize preventative care. This might include routine check-ups, health education, and wellness initiatives.

4. **Palliative Care:** Assist patients with terminal diseases by providing palliative care services. This includes emotional support, pain control, and care coordination with other medical professionals.
5. **Home-Based Primary Care:** Create models for home-based primary care that enable clients to receive primary care services in their homes. This may lessen the need for hospital visits and increase access to treatment.

Accepting Advances in Technology

Keeping up with technological developments may help you increase operational effectiveness and care quality.

1. **Artificial Intelligence (AI):** Apply AI to enhance decision-making and the provision of healthcare. AI is useful for activities like care plan customization, predictive analytics, and scheduling.
2. **Mobile applications:** Create your own or use pre-existing applications to help families, clients, and caregivers communicate with one another. Reminders, access to health information, and real-time updates may all be obtained via apps.
3. **Robotics:** Examine how robotics might help with duties related to providing care. Robotic tools may improve the standard of care by helping with activities like lifting, moving about, and providing company.
4. **Internet of Things (IoT):** Utilize IoT gadgets to build smart home settings that

improve customers' comfort and safety. This may include security systems, health monitoring equipment, and intelligent lighting.

5. **Virtual Reality (VR):** Include VR in your therapy and rehabilitation care plans. Virtual reality (VR) offers immersive experiences to complement both cognitive and physical treatment.

Growing Your Company

Finding Room for Development

The key to growing your home care company is recognizing and seizing development opportunities.

1. **industry research research:** To find trends, opportunities, and gaps in your industry, do in-depth market research.

Examine market trends, rival products, and customer requirements to determine opportunities for expansion.

2. **Service Diversification:** Increase the breadth of services you provide to better serve your customers' varied demands. This may include offering wellness initiatives, assistance for long-term illnesses, and other specialized care services.

3. **Geographic Expansion:** Take into account extending your offerings to new regions. Determine the level of competition and demand in possible new markets, then create a plan of attack to penetrate them.

4. **Strategic Partnerships:** Establish strategic alliances with corporations, community groups, and other healthcare

providers. Working together may expand your clientele and improve the services you provide.

5. **Franchising:** To grow your company more quickly, look into franchising options. Through franchising, you may makemake use of the assets and labor of franchisees while leveraging your own brand and business plan.

Effectively Scaling Operations

Effectively scaling your operations is essential to controlling expansion and maintaining the standard of service.

1. **Infrastructure Development:** Make investments in infrastructure that fosters expansion,such as modernized computer systems, roomier offices, and improved training initiatives.

2. **Standardized Processes:** As you grow, preserve consistency and quality by creating standardized processes and procedures. Making thorough operating manuals and training materials is part of this.
3. **Staffing and Training:** To accommodate growing demand, hire and train more employees. Make sure that, in order to maintain high levels of care, new hires get thorough training and assistance.
4. **Quality Control:** As you expand, make sure that strict quality control procedures are in place to guarantee that care standards are maintained. This covers procedures for customer feedback, performance reviews, and routine audits.
5. **Financial Management:** Make sure you have enough cash on hand to sustain

expansion. This entails raising capital, controlling cash flow, and setting aside money for expansion-related costs.

Acquisitions and Mergers

Increasing your market presence and growing your home care company may be accomplished via strategic mergers and acquisitions, or M&A.

1. **Identify Possible Targets:** Determine possible targets for an acquisition or merger that fit with your company's objectives and core values. Take into account elements including competitive positioning, financial stability, and cultural fit.
2. **Due Diligence:** Evaluate a merger or acquisition's feasibility and possible dangers by conducting in-depth due diligence. This includes assessing

operational skills, legal issues, and financial figures.

3. **Integration Planning:** To guarantee a seamless transfer, create a comprehensive integration strategy. This entails informing employees and customers about changes as well as coordinating systems, procedures, and cultural norms.

4. **Maximize Synergies:** Determine where the merging entities can best work together. This may include pooling resources, cross-selling services, and streamlining processes.

5. **Monitor and adjust:** Keep an eye on the combined or purchased entity's performance and make any required modifications. Review operational and financial indicators on a regular basis to

make sure the merger or acquisition is producing the anticipated advantages.

By concentrating on marketing

You may attain growth and innovation in the home care sector by adopting creative care solutions, strategically growing your company, and developing your business. By using these tactics, you can adapt to the changing demands of your clientele, keep up with market developments, and set up your home care company for long-term success. You may create a successful and cutting-edge home care company that provides your customers with outstanding care by committing to excellence and always striving for improvement.

CHAPTER 5

MAINTAINING GREATNESS

Ongoing Enhancement and Modification

Establishing a Continuous Improvement Culture

Promoting a culture of continual improvement is essential to preserving quality in the home care sector. This entails motivating every team member to continuously look for methods to improve their abilities, workflows, and offerings.

1. **Promote innovation:** Establish a culture where staff members are empowered to make suggestions for enhancements and new ideas. Acknowledge and promote creative thinking, and put in place a

methodical procedure for assessing and approving fresh ideas.

2. **Continuous Education and Training:** Give your employees chances for professional growth and training on a regular basis. This guarantees that they remain up-to-date with emerging technology and industry best practices. Promote the participation of online courses, seminars, and conferences.

3. **Feedback Mechanisms:** Provide strong channels for workers, customers, and their families to provide feedback. Review this feedback often to find areas that need work and answer any concerns.

4. **Performance Metrics:** Keep an eye on key performance indicators (KPIs) to gauge how well your services are working. Utilize this data to monitor

performance, spot patterns, and discover areas that need improvement. Share these metrics with your team on a regular basis to keep everyone focused on the same objectives.

5. **Continuous Review and Adaptation:** Make sure your procedures, guidelines, and offerings are still applicable and efficient by reviewing them on a regular basis. Be flexible and prepared to adjust in response to criticism and performance information.

Keeping Up with Industry Shifts

The home care sector is always changing due to new developments in technology, modifications to laws, and adjustments in the expectations of clients. Sustaining greatness requires keeping ahead of these developments.

1. **Industry Research:** Keep abreast of innovations and trends in the industry. To remain up-to-date on the newest developments and best practices, attend conferences, join professional groups, and subscribe to industry magazines.
2. **Networking:** Create and preserve connections with other experts in the field. Networking may provide insightful information about new trends, laws, and creative methods. It also creates chances for collaboration and teamwork.
3. **Regulatory Compliance:** Make sure your company complies with all applicable laws and regulations by keeping up with regulatory obligations. Review and update your rules and processes on a regular basis to take regulatory changes into account.

4. **Technological Developments:** Take advantage of emerging technology to raise the caliber and effectiveness of your offerings. This covers automation tools, healthcare, and remote monitoring. Invest in technology that improves the effectiveness of operations and the delivery of services.

5. **Client Preferences:** Keep an eye out for changes to client expectations and preferences. To learn about their wants and preferences, do focus groups and surveys on a regular basis. Make adjustments to your services based on this information to increase customer happiness.

Adjusting to Changing Client Requirements

The expectations and demands of clients might

vary over time. To continue providing high-quality treatment and preserving customer happiness, it is essential to adjust to these changing demands.

1. **Personalized Care Plans:** Update care plans often to take into account your customers' evolving requirements and preferences. Assess their health on a regular basis and include them in the planning of their treatment.
2. **Flexible Services:** Provide services that are adaptable to the demands of your clients. This entails offering several care tiers, specialized services, and flexibility in response to changes in patients' medical circumstances.
3. **Client Communication:** Continue to communicate with clients and their

families in an honest and open manner. Respond to their inquiries and concerns, and keep them updated on any modifications to their care plans.

4. **Input and Modifications:** Continually solicit input from customers and apply it to refine your product. Make sure your services are meeting changing needs by reviewing customer feedback on a regular basis and making the necessary changes.

5. **Proactive Care:** Take a proactive stance toward your care, recognizing possible problems early on and taking action to resolve them. This might involve early intervention techniques, routine health examinations, and preventative care measures.

Durability and Legacy of Leadership

Creating a Durable Effect

Making a long-lasting impression that goes beyond your term in office should be your aim as a leader in the home care sector. This entails laying a solid foundation and cultivating an enduring culture of excellence.

1. **Vision and Values:** Clearly state your company's goals and principles, and make sure they permeate every part of operations. Make sure your team knows about them on a regular basis, and use them as the foundation for all decisions and activities.
2. **Sustainable Practices:** Put into effect long-term success-promoting sustainable business practices. This entails making

investments in the training of employees, upholding strict care guidelines, and cultivating a happy workplace.

3. **Community Engagement:** Build strong connections with the communities you serve. Engage in community engagement, support local activities, and promote your firm as a trusted and important community resource.

4. **Documented Processes:** Develop and record standardized processes and procedures. This promotes continuity and gives a clear foundation for future leaders to follow.

5. **Performance Excellence:** Aim for superiority across the board in your company. Always look for ways to do better and hold yourself to the highest levels of performance and quality.

Guiding the Upcoming Generation of Executives

The next generation of leaders has to be developed and mentored if you want your home care company to succeed in the long run.

1. **Identify Possible Leaders:** Determine which team members have the capacity to assume leadership positions. Seek out people who have a great sense of communication, a dedication to quality work, and a love of providing care.
2. **Offer Growth Opportunities:** Provide chances for leadership growth and career advancement. To boost their abilities and self-assurance, encourage aspiring leaders to take on more tasks and responsibilities.
3. **mentoring programs:** Create mentoring initiatives that match seasoned executives

with up-and-coming executives. This offers an organized method for the transfer of expertise and experience, as well as for the mentoring and assistance of upcoming leaders.

4. **Leadership Development:** Establish an extensive program for developing leaders that covers management, communication, problem-solving, and strategic planning training. To ensure the success of upcoming leaders, provide them with resources and continual assistance.

5. **Empower and Delegate:** Give emerging leaders responsibility and include them in decision-making to help them become more powerful. Give them helpful criticism and encouragement so they may develop and strengthen their leadership

skills.

Examining Your Leadership Development

By reflecting on your leadership experience, you may gain insightful knowledge and advance your leadership development. It also enables you to impart to others the knowledge and insights you have gained.

1. **Self-Assessment:** As a leader, evaluate your strengths and opportunities for development on a regular basis. Think back on your successes, difficulties, and the influence you have had on your customers and team.
2. **Seek Feedback:** To learn more about the opinions of others on your leadership style and efficacy, ask for input from your mentors, peers, and team. Make the

required modifications and enhancements using the input provided here.

3. **Travel Journal:** Write down all of your encounters, difficulties, and victories. Recording your experience may be a useful tool for future leaders and assist you in reflecting on your own development.

4. **Tell Your Story:** Through speeches, writings, or mentoring, share your leadership experiences and learnings with others. Others may be inspired and guided by your experiences as they pursue leadership careers.

5. **Continuous Learning:** Make a commitment to your own personal growth and lifetime learning. Continue to be inquisitive, pursue new information, and have an open mind to fresh viewpoints.

This will support your ongoing development and evolution as a leader.

You may maintain greatness in your home care company by emphasizing ongoing adaptation and improvement, creating a lasting influence, coaching the next generation of leaders, and thinking back on your leadership path. These tactics will support you in adapting to changes in the market, satisfying changing customer demands, and leaving a long-lasting legacy of excellence and innovation. You can guarantee your home care business's long-term success and impact by putting growth and quality first.

CONCLUSION

Your Path to Around-the-Clock Excellence

Now that we have reached the end of our exploration of the complex field of home care leadership, it is time to compile the most important tactics and ideas discussed in this book. "Around-the-Clock Excellence: Winning Strategies for Home Care Business Leaders" aims to provide you with the skills required to manage your company successfully, guaranteeing excellent care and long-term growth. Let's review the key techniques, provide some closing ideas, and provide resources for your further education.

Summary of Crucial Techniques

1. **Understanding the Home Care Environment:**
   Keep up with developments in upcoming technology, regulations, and industry trends.
   Regularly analyze the market to learn about your competitors and spot expansion prospects.
2. **Establishing Your Goals and Vision:**
   Draft a compelling vision statement that serves as the organization's compass.
   Define fundamental principles that represent your dedication to moral behavior and high-quality medical

treatment.

To guide your strategic planning, establish attainable short- and long-term objectives.

3. **Creating a Robust Corporate Culture:**
   Encourage an atmosphere at work where people feel appreciated and that communication is open.

   Adopt employee engagement and retention measures, such as offering career development opportunities and recognition programs.

4. **Effective Styles of Leadership:**
   Recognize your preferred leadership style and modify it to fit different circumstances for maximum impact.

   Set a good example by acting with honesty, compassion, and a dedication to perfection.

5. **Finding and Bringing in Talent:**

    Adopt best practices for selecting and onboarding outstanding professionals, such as extensive screening and onboarding procedures.

    To improve the abilities and expertise of your staff, make continuous training and development program investments.

6. **Sustainability and Financial Management:**

    Create a thorough financial strategy that addresses cash flow and budgeting.

    Examine your possibilities for investments and financing to help with business expansion and sustainability.

7. **Maximizing Efficiency of Operations:**

    Simplify procedures and make use of technology to improve operational effectiveness.

Use quality control procedures to keep an eye on and enhance performance.

8. **Strategies for Client-Centered Care:**
Pay close attention to comprehending and fulfilling each client's particular demands.
to maintain high standards, provide individualized service, and track customer satisfaction on a regular basis.

9. **Problem-Solving and Crisis Management:**
Create a solid crisis response strategy to manage crises well.
Use proactive problem-solving strategies and draw lessons from previous setbacks to enhance future reactions.

10. **Business Development and Marketing:**
Create a marketing plan that is appealing and emphasizes your special selling point.

To draw in new business, make good use of digital marketing tools and establish robust networks of referrals.

11. **New Approaches to Healthcare:**

    Adopt new technologies like remote monitoring and telemedicine.

    Investigate novel care approaches and keep coming up with fresh ideas to remain ahead of market trends.

12. **Growing Your Enterprise:**

    Seek chances for development and expansion, including new service offerings and regional expansion.

    Strategically plan and carry out mergers and acquisitions to improve your market position.

13. **Ongoing Enhancement and Modification:**

    Foster a culture of continual improvement

where changes are welcomed and feedback is appreciated.

Remain flexible in response to changing customer demands and market shifts.

Final Thoughts and Motivation

Running a home care agency is a rewarding and difficult endeavor. The techniques presented in this book provide a road map for overcoming industrial challenges and achieving excellence around-the-clock. Keep in mind that leadership is a journey rather than a destination as you put these tactics into practice. Relentless learning, adjustment, and development are necessary for long-term success.

In order to shape the future of your business and the kind of care you provide, your leadership position is essential. Accept the difficulties with a proactive attitude and a positive outlook.

Honor your accomplishments, draw lessons from your failures, and always prioritize the welfare of your customers.

Maintain your commitment to your vision and beliefs, surround yourself with a strong team, and cultivate a culture of creativity and cooperation. Your example of leadership will motivate others and have a knock-on effect that affects not just your company but the whole home care industry.

Resources for Continued Education

It's critical to maintain your commitment to professional development and continuous learning if you want to remain on your path to greatness. These are some tools to help you:

Associations for Professionals:

Become a member of trade groups like the

Home Care Association of America (HCAOA) or the National Association for Home Care & Hospice (NAHC). These groups provide informative events, networking opportunities, and useful resources.

Virtual Programs and Accreditations:

Examine online programs for leadership, home care techniques, and healthcare administration certificates. Numerous relevant courses are available on websites such as Coursera, Udemy, and LinkedIn Learning.

Workshops and Conferences:

To keep informed about the newest trends, technology, and best practices, attend industry conferences and seminars. Additionally, networking opportunities with other industry leaders and specialists are offered by these gatherings.

Research and Reading:

Read books, journals, and industry magazines to stay informed. To stay up-to-date with the latest news and updates, subscribe to newsletters and blogs from reliable sources.

Networks of Peers and Mentors:

Look for mentors and connect with peers to learn from and get advice from seasoned leaders. Peer interactions and experience sharing may provide insightful viewpoints and helpful encouragement.

Ongoing Input and Enhancement:

Establish a procedure for getting ongoing input from your employees and customers. Utilize this input to pinpoint areas that need work and modify your tactics and procedures as needed.

In summary, achieving round-the-clock greatness is a lifelong process of development and education. Through the use of the tactics discussed in this book and a dedication to continuous improvement, you can take your home care company to unprecedented levels of achievement. Accept the difficulties, acknowledge the successes, and never waver in your commitment to provide top-notch care. Your team, the community at large, and your customers' lives can all be significantly improved by your leadership.

117

www.ingramcontent.com/pod-product-compliance
Lightning Source LLC
Chambersburg PA
CBHW071522220526
45472CB00003B/1117